VIVIEN G. SWAN, B.A.

POTTERY
IN ROMAN BRITAIN

SHIRE ARCHAEOLOGY

TITLES IN THE SHIRE ARCHAEOLOGY SERIES
Anglo-Saxon Jewellery Ronald Jessup
Bronze Age Metalwork in England and Wales Nancy Langmaid
Flint Implements of the Old Stone Age Peter Timms
Pottery in Roman Britain Vivien G. Swan

Published by
SHIRE PUBLICATIONS LTD
Cromwell House, Church Street, Princes Risborough,
Aylesbury, Buckinghamshire, U.K.

Series Editor: James Dyer

Copyright © Vivien G. Swan, 1975

ISBN 0 85263 268 1
Library of Congress Catalog Card Number: 74-83359

First published 1975

Printed by C. I. Thomas & Sons (Haverfordwest) Ltd.

Contents

Cover illustration: New Forest painted flagon (photograph by K. Grinstead).

List of plates and figures

Preface

This book is intended as an outline to pottery forms and fabrics most widely distributed in Roman Britain, and the development of major production centres. Specialist terms (such as may be found on museum labels or excavation reports) which are not explained in the text or by illustrations, will be found in the glossary (p. 6). All dates given are AD: centuries are mostly indicated by simple Roman numerals alone. In common with standard practice, pottery has been drawn at a scale of one-quarter with the external elevation on the right and a thickness section on the left (as if a quadrant had been cut away). Thus, external decoration appears on the right of the central dividing line, and internal features on the left.

The writer would like to acknowledge assistance from the following: Catherine Johns (British Museum), Bryan Blake (Derby Museum), Peter Saunders (Salisbury Museum), the Yorkshire Museum (York), Christopher Young (Department of the Environment), and colleagues in the Royal Commission on Historical Monuments (England). In particular, I owe much to the work of the following: John Gillam (University of Newcastle upon Tyne) on northern material, Kevin Greene (University of Newcastle upon Tyne) on early fine wares, Mrs Katherine Hartley on mortaria, and above all Dr Graham Webster, who first encouraged my interest in Romano-British coarse pottery. Thanks are due to Andrew Selkirk (*Current Archaeology*), the Derby Museum, the Guildford Museum, the Oxford Archaeological Excavation Committee, the Rheinisches Landesmuseum, Trier, the Royal Commission on Historical Monuments (England), and the Trustees of the British Museum, for permission to reproduce photographs, to Ken Grinstead for the cover illustration and Plates 27, 28, 30-33, and to Nick Griffiths for drawing the kiln reconstruction.

Glossary

Barbotine: relief decoration executed by trailing semi-liquid clay squeezed through the end of some implement into a finished vessel before firing, a process identical to icing a cake (Plates 18 and 19).

Burnishing: a smooth (sometimes shiny) area of a pot obtained by the pressure or rubbing action of a tool applied immediately prior to firing.

Carination: a sharp inward change of angle in the body of a vessel.

Fabric or paste: the prepared clay with which a vessel was manufactured.

Foot-ring: a low raised ring added to the base of a vessel to aid stability (Fig. III, no. 18).

Rouletting: incised decoration made by a toothed wheel or roller applied while the vessel was turning on the potter's wheel (Fig. X, no. 58).

Slip, colour-coat, paint: the term *slip* refers to both a solution of clay and water (with or without added colorants) into which a vessel could be dipped, and the resultant finish after firing. When such a slip is made darker (by means of added minerals) than the paste of the vessel which it covers, it is called a *colour-coat*. The term *paint* is used in the sense of a thick slip (white or coloured) applied decoratively (by brush or other implement) to the finished surface of a pot prior to firing (Plate 23).

1

Introduction

Pottery is undoubtedly the most common archaeological material surviving on Roman sites, and its study is important for two main reasons: firstly as a chronological indicator when other datable objects such as coins are lacking, and secondly, for the information it can provide on trade and communications when examined distributionally.

When the Roman army invaded Britain in 43, they found a number of potting traditions already established. On the one hand, the inhabitants particularly of Kent, Essex, and Hertfordshire, who had close links with the continent (Belgicized), were importing and mass-producing wheel-thrown, good-quality pottery and distributing it on a considerable scale, and on the other hand, elsewhere, pottery was hand-made, mostly on a comparatively small scale and, with a few exceptions, usually sold fairly locally. There were even some areas in Britain whose Iron Age people do not seem to have made pottery (aceramic), but must have used vessels of wood or leather only. The Romans were adaptable, and so while many new types of vessel were introduced, such as flagons (Figs. I and III) and mortaria (Figs. VI and VII), some British Iron Age native forms, such as the handled mug or tankard (Fig. IV, no. 25) were soon assimilated.

At first, therefore, the invading army was obliged to bring with it some of its own pottery and immediately to encourage native potters to supply it: evidence also suggests that some Gallic potters came over in the army's wake to take advantage of the situation. Similarly, capitalists would have arrived, ready to finance and expand suitable potteries with an eye on obtaining contracts to supply the Roman army. Such a contract was one of the most decisive factors for the development of any manufacturing centre; it could raise a workshop from purely local status to that of a major industrial organization. Although no military contract-documents relating to pottery survive for anywhere in the Roman empire, it is clear, from the combined local and non-local distribution of many specialist products, that such agreements must have existed. In a few instances the actual legions or auxiliaries seem to have undertaken or directly supervised the production of pottery in Britain (p. 9), for example at Longthorpe (Peterborough), Brampton (Cumbria), Holt (Clwyd), and Grimscar (Huddersfield), where it was linked with tile manufacture, and at Usk (Gwent), where evidence suggests the presence of potters from the Rhineland and Danube provinces. The practice was not normal after early II and the works-depot at Quernmore, supplying pottery and tiles to the fort at Lancaster in III is, at present, the only exception.

While the major industries were primarily concerned with supplying the army (sometimes from a considerable distance), and tended to concentrate on specialist vessels (for example mortaria and flagons), many smaller potteries of comparatively local significance flourished, and were the main suppliers of the civil markets. Some of these were probably initially set up to supply military units, and when the troops moved north, they were reduced to local status only; whatever the circumstances, most major settlements would have had their own local pottery. Their distinctive products, mostly kitchen wares, were often influenced by local Iron Age traditions and many items continued to be hand-made or partly hand-made throughout the Roman period. These workshops manufactured perhaps between 70 and 80 per cent of all the pottery in Roman Britain, and except in Wales and the north-west (where no native potting tradition existed), most probably never traded their wares more than ten to fifteen miles. This helps to explain the great diversity of wares from region to region.

The pottery types, fashions, and production-centres discussed below (except mortaria and regional wares) have been dealt with in chronological order of their first appearance; however, some survived much longer than others and overlap later introductions. Other products underwent more rapid change, and tend therefore to be more valuable for dating.

2
A.D. *c*. 43 to *c*. 150

The imports and commercial production in the southern part of the province were geared almost entirely to military requirements up to *c*. 70 AD, when civilian markets emerged. By late I to early II, when it became clear that Wales and the north were garrisoned on a permanent basis, there began a tendency for major manufacturers to move nearer their main consumers; for example by 150 the southern centres for mortaria, Kent and Verulamium, had declined, and the Midland factories, Oxford and Hartshill/Mancetter, had replaced them in importance (p. 14).

Varnished ware. Among the pottery imported by the army from 43 to *c*.70 was a range of thin-walled *colour-coated* vessels, known collectively as varnished ware, and produced at several sources on the Continent, particularly near *Lyons* (France). They include small cups, and beakers in a pale greenish-cream *fabric*, with a glossy brownish *slip* and decoration in the form of applied scales (Plate 1), roundels with raspberry-like impressions (Fig. I, no. 2), *rough-cast* (Fig. I, no. 3) or rustication (Plate 1).

Lead-glazed wares also circulated with the army from *c*. 43 to 70; they included a range of fine thin-walled cups, flagons, or jars, some with moulded or applied decoration (Plate 3) or *barbotine* dots (Fig. II, no. 15), 'hair-pin' loops, and covered with a yellowish-green vitreous surface. A number of production centres in the Allier Valley (including *St Rémy-en-Rollat*) were probable sources.

Lead-glazed wares were very occasionally manufactured in Britain, particularly in late I to early II, perhaps under the aegis of the army, as at *Little Chester* (Derby), *Holt* (Clwyd) the tilery of the Twentieth Legion (Plate 4), and possibly also at *Chichester*, Sussex (Fig. II, no. 14).

Mica-dusted or mica-gilt ware. Alongside the frequent imitation (in pottery) of metal vessel-*forms* in the Roman empire was an attempt (probably in Gaul and the Rhineland) to obtain a gold or bronze metallic *finish* by coating brown or buff vessels with a wash containing innumerable specks of yellow mica, a process termed *mica-dusting*. Such jars and bowls (Plate 2, and Fig. II, nos. 6-11) were imported into Britain

in mid I, and soon imitated here, particularly for the army; a kiln at
Gloucester dates to the 70s. The fashion scarcely outlasted I.

Gallo-Belgic wares were already being shipped into Britain, and were
manufactured in the *Verulamium* and *Colchester* areas before 43,
processes greatly stimulated by the Roman army; this resulted in a
widespread distribution south of the Fosse Way. These fine, polished,
grey-black vessels (*Terra Nigra*) and orange-coated cream to buff vessels
(*Terra Rubra*) included a standardized range of cups, dishes, and shallow
platters (Plate 5, and Fig. III, nos. 18-20) with *foot-rings*, and often
bearing the *potter's name-stamp*. While the fashion for Terra Rubra
scarcely survived the 50s, Terra Nigra continued until the 70s, and coarser
imitations were probably being made down to the end of I.

   An allied range of barrel-shaped *butt-beakers* and straight-sided *girth-
beakers* (Plate 5, and Fig. III, nos. 16, and 17), decorated with fine
rouletting and horizontal grooving at intervals, were similarly imitated.

Amphorae (Plate 16), large two-handled containers of wine and oil, etc.,
were imported throughout the Roman period for their contents only.
Their varying shapes reflected differences in origin rather than date.

Samian ware or Terra Sigillata. This distinctive, glossy, red-coated, mass-
produced tableware, often relief-decorated, flooded into Britain after 43.
Except for a handful of sherds from *Arretium* (Italy), the British imports
were manufactured in *South Gaul*, in centres such as *La Graufesenque*
(France), until c. 110; the *Central Gaulish factories*, notably *Lezoux* (near
Clermont Ferrand) then took over as the main source to Britain (together
with a few smaller *East Gaulish*, Rhineland potteries), until early in III
when the traffic ceased. A range of cups, bowls (Plate 9), platters, jars,
mortaria, and even inkwells is known. Both plain and decorated vessels
often bear the name-stamp of the potters or workshops (Plate 7) and may
be fairly closely dated. Most decorated samian vessels were made in
moulds (Plate 8), impressed with stamps of mythological figures, animals,
birds, scenes from everyday life, and foliage-trails; thus it is often possible
to assign a vessel to a particular potter from the style or *decorative details*.
Rouletting, barbotine, and incised 'cut-glass' style decoration and
'marbled' and black-coated (*black samian*) vessels also occur. The
numerous standardized vessel-forms have been given numbers for easy
identification, mostly by an archaeologist named *Dragendorff*
(abbreviated to Drag. or Dr.).

Colchester samian. An attempt was made to manufacture samian at Colchester in the second half of II, but it seems to have been short-lived and vessels only sold locally.

Argonne ware (see p. 20 and Fig. XI, no. 70).

Early imitation of samian. The popularity of samian was such that in late I and early II several factories in southern England (for example West Stow, Suffolk) began to produce grey or black imitations of some samian bowl forms, often in fabrics in the Terra Nigra tradition with a polished surface, and usually termed *London ware*. They were decorated with rouletting, impressed stamps, groups of vertical incised lines or compass-scribed circles (Plate 10).

Orange ware vessels, also imitating samian forms, were manufactured in late I-II at such centres as Little Chester (Derby), York, Caerleon (*Caerleon ware*), and Gloucester and the Severn Valley, largely for military markets.

Late imitation samian (see p. 18).

The flagon. A narrow-mouthed globular vessel-type new to Britain in 43; the earliest examples were probably either imported or produced locally for the army. One universal characteristic of I and II was a light coloured fabric. If available clays fired too dark, flagon manufacturers coated them with a pale slip. In general, flagons became smaller in III and IV.

Hofheim flagons (Fig. I, no. 1), imported or manufactured here for the army c. 43-70, had almost cylindrical necks, out-curved lips (triangular in section), and might be single or double-handled.

Ring-neck flagons. A most common type, with a mouth-piece of multiple superimposed rings; in mid I the neck-top was more or less vertical (Fig. III, no. 21), but the rings soon began to splay outwards. During II the top ring-lip thickened and protruded, while the lower rings became fewer (Fig. IX, no. 53), or even degenerated into mere grooving; the square handles of I also developed a more rounded profile.

Flanged-neck flagons (Plate 32, and Fig. VIII, no. 44) occur in a variety of fabrics mostly colour-coated (see Nene Valley and New Forest wares) in III and IV.

Other common first- and early second-century forms introduced in 43, or developed shortly after, and widely manufactured in England include:

Carinated bowls (Fig. II, no. 11) with flat or grooved (*reeded*) rims, initially imported by the army, who encouraged local production; they terminated *c.* 150 in the south, but a little earlier in the north, probably as a result of the influx of black-burnished bowls (see p. 42), whose early forms they clearly influenced.

Poppy-head beakers (Plate 6). Shaped like poppy seed-heads and developed in Britain from Gallo-Belgic prototypes; a grey or black polished fabric was normal with panels of barbotine dots. Current from *c.* 60 to 190 in southern England, examples arrived later in the north (*c.* 120-90). Some may have been shipped up the East Coast from potteries on the Upchurch Marshes (Kent) in the Thames Estuary.

Rustic or rusticated ware (Plate 14). A fashion normally associated with grey jars (probably for cooking), in which a very thick slip, applied after the vessels were thrown, was worked up with the fingers into rough knobs, parallel ridges, or spidery encrustations. A continental form popular with the army, it was made in England between 50 and 120; after 70 production and distribution tended to be geared to the northern garrisons, until it was superseded there in the 120s by the influx of black-burnished cooking pots (see p. 13).

Rough-cast ware included a range of colour-coated *indented* or bag-shaped beakers with delicately moulded (*cornice*) rims (Plate 22, and Fig. IX); the body surface was sprinkled with tiny particles of dried clay. Perhaps initially produced to meet army demands, when the importation of most *varnished ware* more globular prototypes (Fig. I, no. 3) ceased *c.* 70, they lasted until late II. The fabric is usually orange-brown, and in the north the colour-coating tends to be purple-brown on the earlier specimens and yellowish-orange on the later.

Severn Valley wares originated in about mid I, perhaps initially in connection with supplies for the legionary fortresses at Wroxeter and Gloucester. Jars, tankards and bowls (Fig. IV, nos. 22-25) in various fabrics, usually hard light buff-orange, with burnished areas or lines, emanated from many centres such as *Shepton Mallet* (Somerset), *Perry Barr* (Birmingham), the *Gloucester* area (where it is called *Glevum ware*), and a large factory near *Malvern* (Worcestershire) and continued into IV.

They were marketed mainly in the Severn Valley and adjacent areas, but a small amount was supplied to turrets and milecastles on a sector of Hadrian's Wall from *c.* 120-40.

Black-burnished ware. A military contract was undoubtedly the cause of the sudden rise to prominence of this type of pottery. Two fabrics are distinguishable: one (*Category I*) with its origins among the Iron Age (*Durotrigian*) peoples of Dorset is black and gritty, and was hand-made and *burnished* in facets; the other (*Category II*) is greyish finer, and wheel-thrown, with a silky more regular surface. Its manufacture probably began later in eastern England, in imitation of Category I forms. About 120, the manufacturers of Category I, whose products had hitherto found their main markets in Dorset and south Wiltshire, contracted to supply quantities to the army on Hadrian's Wall and its hinterland; about 140, Category II vessels were the subject of a similar contract. Subsequently these arrangements existed until *c.* 250, when Category II vessels no longer reached the north. Category I products continued to be supplied there until after *c.* 367, when they were ousted by the Huntcliff and Crambeck kitchen wares (p. 20). Elsewhere from II to the end of IV, Category I vessels were fairly common, except in East Anglia and the south-east, where they presumably met with greater competition from the Category II factories.

The standard range of black-burnished vessel-forms was fairly uniform, with only minor variations from fabric to fabric; they were widely imitated by many local potteries over the whole of Britain. The thin-walled *cooking-pots* were clearly for use over a fire or oven, and the development of their shape and decoration is a useful chronological guide. In II they were squat, with short necks and upward flaring rims (Fig. V, no. 27); burnishing occurred just inside the rim and on the exterior, except for a broad central band of lightly incised *acute-angled lattice* decoration. In III and IV, vessels were more elongated, with a longer neck and a rim projecting outwards, well beyond the body of the pot (Plate 11, and Fig. V, no. 28); the lattice, by now *obtuse-angled*, was confined to a very much narrower bank, often terminated above by a horizontally burnished line or groove.

The bowl in II was a carinated vessel, with a flattened rim, and a band of acute-angled lattice (Fig. V, no. 29). By *c.* 180 an incipient band developed on the more hooked rim; the version of late III-IV was proportionally deeper, with a pronounced bead rim and flange (Plate 11, and Fig. V, no. 30).

A simple shallow platter, often referred to as a '*dog-dish*', was also popular (Plate 11, and Fig. V, no. 31) and tended to be more common in late III-IV.

3
Mortaria

These general purpose mixing-bowls, newly introduced by the army, had heavy rims for easy gripping and lifting, grits on the interior surface to reinforce the vessel and aid mixing, and (often) pouring spouts (Plate 13). Their production was always concentrated in the hands of specialist potters.

The early south-east factories. At first the Roman army had to import their mortaria from Italy and Gaul (Fig. VI, no. 33), but by between 60 and 70 several factories specializing in these vessels had grown to importance in south-east England supplying both the army further north, and the more Romanized settlements in the south (for example, London). Of particular importance were potteries south of Verulamium (St Albans, Hertfordshire) including *Brockley Hill* (Greater London) and *Radlett* (Hertfordshire), and kilns at *Colchester*, and somewhere in *Kent;* their mortaria, in cream or buff fabrics, had large hooked rims, well-made spouts, and tiny flint gritting spread over the interior and rim (Plate 12, and Fig. VI, nos. 34 and 35). The potters, such as Q. Valerius Veranius, who seems to have moved his workshop from Bavai in Gallia Belgica (Belgium) to Kent, and Matugenus, who worked at Brockley Hill, often impressed their name-stamps or trademarks across the rim near the spout (Plate 12); this tradition was carried on in other production centres until the end of II.

The Hartshill and Mancetter factories. The south-east workshops gradually declined in importance early in II; but by *c.* 100 a new industry, which was to predominate for almost three centuries, had been set up in the area of *Hartshill* and *Mancetter*, near Nuneaton (Warwickshire). A study of fabrics and stamps on mortaria has suggested that at least one potter, G. Attius Marinus, previously at Colchester and Radlett, migrated to Hartshill/Mancetter in *c.* 100.

The vast industrial complex with its numerous potters soon became one of the main suppliers of mortaria to the north, particularly to the army, and in addition dominated the Midland market. Characteristic were vessels in a distinctive fine white hard 'pipe-clay' fabric, with medium-sized red-brown grits, applied on the interior only. By the middle of II the current fashion was for smaller flanges, less hooked and more flaring, and more prominent rounded rims (Fig. VII, nos. 39 and 40).

Towards the end of II, coinciding with a streamlining and

intensification of production, the potters discontinued name-stamping and began to manufacture *hammer-head* rims; these were sometimes decorated with horizontal grooving (reeding), or after *c.* 230 *painted* with groups of vertical stripes (Fig. VII, no. 41). Large-scale distribution continued until the last quarter of IV, when it was reduced to a local scale as a result of competition from the Crambeck kilns (see p. 20).

Second-century centres in northern England. Several other manufacturers achieved success with the northern garrisons, particularly potters centred on Corbridge, Doncaster, Brampton (Norfolk), and around *Lincoln,* and a group at *Wilderspool,* Cheshire (Fig. VI, no. 36) and *Carlisle;* some *Colchester* workshops even shipped their wares up the east coast to the Antonine Wall (Scotland) (Fig. IX, no. 54).

Second-century centres in southern England and Wales. A large industry developed around *Oxford* (for example kilns at Cowley); between *c.* 120 and 160, the potters impressed mostly illegible trademark-stamps on mortaria in a fine cream fabric, often with a pink or orange tinge (Fig. VII, no. 37); the distinctive multicoloured (predominantly pink), translucent quartz internal grits were the hallmark of Oxford mortaria both then and later (p. 18).

Serving Wales, the Marches, and the Bristol Channel area in II were several centres. One, probably in the area of *Caerleon* (Gwent), and perhaps initially associated with the Second Augusta Legion there, made smooth red-coated mortaria, sometimes illegibly stamped, and gritted with white quartz.

Another factory, probably in the vicinity of Cirencester, produced mortaria in a coarse orange fabric with a cream slip and grits of flint and pink quartz from late II to late III at least. The earlier types were sometimes impressed with unusual trade-stamps such as rosettes; flagons and jars also probably emanated from the same source, and were marketed mainly in Wiltshire, Gloucestershire and Somerset.

A group of potters, probably working in the *Wroxeter* (Salop) area between 110 and 160, marketed rather gritty cream-orange vessels; an orangey slip and grey and mixed grits were characteristic.

Some of the so-called 'Raetian' mortaria may also have been made in the Wroxeter region in the second half of II; these are orange, with lugs, cut-out spouts and a reddish gloss (Fig. VI, no. 36); however, 'Raetians' were mainly produced by the Wilderspool workshops which had close connections.

The late centres. See under Nene Valley, Oxford, Crambeck and New Forest.

4

The mid second century onwards

By *c.* 140 the impact on the pottery industry of the early exotic types imported by the army had diminished considerably, and although there continued to be links with the continent, types in general became more insular. The growth, too, of civilian markets had encouraged the establishment of regional industries supplying the local settlements (see p. 21).

Soon after 150, there began in Britain large-scale production of a great variety of fine, sometimes elaborate colour-coated table-ware—a fashion which was to last until the end of IV and which may ultimately have been instrumental in the decline of samian imports to Britain. The two main manufacturing centres, *Colchester* and the *Lower Nene Valley* seem to have commenced almost simultaneously *c.* 145-50, and there are hints of the presence of immigrant potters from the Rhineland.

The Lower Nene Valley. There had been pottery manufacture in the area since mid I, when workshops were set up to supply the vexillation-fortress of Longthorpe, and similar kilns at various Upper Nene Valley sites also potted largely for military requirements. The industrial complex of mid II onwards spreads for several miles between Wansford and Peterborough, along the north bank of the River Nene (Cambridgeshire), with its centre at the Roman town of *Durobrivae* (Water Newton). Often called *castor ware*, after the parish in which it was first recognized, the main products, in a fine whitish fabric, comprise a great variety of forms both plain and decorated. They include flagons, *'castor boxes'* (Fig. VIII, no. 42), and indented, globular, and bag-shaped beakers (Plate 20, and Fig. VIII, no. 47), many of which have a wide distribution almost all over Britain. Most famous are the *'hunt cups'* with their lively running animals *en barbotine* (Plate 18), and vessels with similarly executed barbotine or painted floral-scrolls (Plate 20). Zones of rouletting and applied scales (Plate 20) were also popular, and the colour-coats range from dark-brown to orange, fawn, or olive green. Many of the wares continued in production until the end of IV, together with a range of culinary vessels for more local markets. Mortaria too were manufactured in III and IV (Plate 21, and Fig. VIII, no. 46), and may be distinguished by their black iron-stone grits; in III-IV the Nene Valley potters followed the fashion for producing *late imitation samian* (Fig. VIII, no. 45) and *late painted parchment wares* (p. 18).

Colchester had remained a major pottery manufacturing centre since the Conquest, when the Roman army (and probably also capitalist speculators following in its wake) encouraged large-scale production of Gallo-Belgic forms, imitation of imported fine wares, and probably mortaria as well (p. 14).

Shortly before mid II (among many other products) the Colchester kilns began to make a range of fine table wares generally similar to the Nene Valley products (Plate 22, and Fig. IX). Characteristic is an orange fabric with red, brown, or black colour-coats. Barbotine motifs on some beakers include public shows (Plate 19), and hunting scenes, phallic symbols, and strange, perhaps Celtic, masked men engaged in ritual mysteries! A thorough study of the distribution of the wares outside East Anglia is well overdue; no doubt aside from London, military contracts provided the main outlets, since rough-cast beakers from Colchester are known on the Antonine Wall—presumably shipped there with the mortaria of II. Some pottery production probably continued at Colchester until the end of IV.

There were other centres known to be making colour-coated wares in II and III (for example, *Pakenham* and *Homersfield,* Suffolk, *Great Casterton,* Leics, and *South Carlton,* Lincs.), but the distribution of their products was probably fairly localized.

'Rhenish' ware. Vessels in this thin orange fabric, often with grey core and a lustrous black or bronze colour-coat, were imported from the Rhineland or Moselle from *c.* 180 to mid III, and have a wide distribution, particularly in the north-east, where they were probably shipped direct. Vessel forms included rouletted indented beakers, and bulbous beakers decorated *en barbotine* or with white *paint.* Well-known are the *'motto-beakers'* (Plate 23), in which the painted scrolls were combined with ornately lettered words forming phrases such as *DA MERUM* (Give [me] pure wine!), and *BIBE* (Drink up!), and many other less refined instructions! Some of the Central Gaulish samian factories, notably Lezoux, exported to Britain black colour-coated vessels almost indistinguishable from Rhenish ware. The fabric, however, tends to be micaceous and barbotine leaf and dot decoration is particularly characteristic.

5

Late third- and fourth- century pottery

Because of the lack of closely dated deposits on the northern frontier in the first half of III, there is some doubt which pottery should be assigned to this period. However, by late III a number of trends can be clearly distinguished: most notably *(a) late imitation samian wares* and *(b) late painted parchment wares* (for main production centres of both, see below and p. 22):

> *(a)* is also known as *pseudo-samian*. The fabrics varied according to their centre of manufacture, but normally had a reddish colour-coat. Vessels imitated, both in shape and decoration, the latest samian arriving in Britain, or the colour-coated wares which evolved from it in the Rhineland and Britain. The normal range comprised bowls, cups, and mortaria. *Decoration was no longer by means of stamped moulds (see samian, p. 10), but was impressed directly into the pot itself.*
>
> *(b)* comprises a range of table-ware, mostly bowls, in pale fabrics which have simple red-brown painted decoration.

In general, there were inclined to be fewer, but larger main production centres in IV and this may have contributed to a more rapid breakdown of the pottery industry in V (p. 23).

The Oxford late potteries. Although there had been kilns in the region of Oxford since II (p. 15), it was not until mid III that large-scale distribution of table-wares was achieved. Of these, by far the most important was *late imitation samian* often in a pink-orange micaceous fabric with a pinkish-red slip. Impressed *rosettes, demi-rosettes* (Plate 31), *comb-stamping,* (Fig. X, no. 56), and horizontal and curvilinear rouletting are well known. In addition to the more exotic shapes (Fig. X, no. 57), vessels imitated samian forms Drag. 31, 38, 45 (mortarium) (Plate 28) and also 36 with white-painted scrolls in place of barbotine on the rim (Fig. X, no. 55). Distribution was almost universal south of the Trent.

The *parchment wares* from these factories (for example, Headington) were thinly distributed over the same area; characteristic was a fine white powdery fabric, often with a pinkish core with red or brown painted decoration. A carinated bowl (Plate 26), with painted lines on the exterior of the rim and carination, and patterns such as concentric circles on the interior, was the most popular vessel.

Also made in the same fabric were *mortaria* of typical mid-third to fourth-century forms (Plate 29, and Fig. X, no. 61), with prominent rims and rolled-over or sub-square flanges; these were very widely distributed from mid III to early V.

The New Forest potteries produced *late imitation samian* ware in a cream-buff fabric, with a brownish-orange slip. Some vessel-forms and decorative techniques were shared with the Oxford workshops, for example the imitation of forms Drag. 31, 38 (Fig. XI, no. 68), and 45, rosette stamping (Plate 31), and white painted decoration. However these wares were of comparatively local importance, and many of the Oxford counterparts have been wrongly assigned to this source.

New Forest *parchment ware* is sandy, off-white and rough to feel, with red or orange painted designs. Most popular was an internally flanged bowl, painted inside with bands of concentric wavy lines and circles (Plate 27). *Mortaria* too occur in this fabric, recognizable by their internal grey and white grits of crushed flints; in conjunction with prominent *bead-rims*, their flanges may be plain, simply reeded, or decorated with stabbing or an incised wavy line (Fig. XI, no. 62). Consumption was largely confined to Hampshire, Wiltshire, and Dorset.

The well-known *fine colour-coated*, often hard *table-wares* (Plate 32, and Fig. XI) were clearly the most important products from late III to early V, concentrated in the area immediately adjacent to the kilns, and thinly distributed over much of England south of the Thames. The fabrics varied from buff to grey, and the colour-coats from matt red to lustrous purple, depending on whether they were fired to a comparatively low or high temperature. Indented and bulbous beakers, small bowls, and flagons were popular, sometimes decorated with repeating geometric motifs in white paint or incised concentric circles (Fig. XI, no. 67). Grey culinary wares were also made for local consumers (Plate 30, and Fig. IX, no. 69).

A simple chronological framework has recently begun to emerge for Oxfordshire and New Forest products; it seems likely that the earliest imitation samian vessels, appearing in mid to late III, were those whose profiles most closely copied the latest common Gaulish plain samian forms to reach Britain, such as Drag. 31, 33, 36, 38 and 45. The fourth century probably saw increasing elaboration; the practice of stamping appears to have commenced about mid IV or shortly before, and at about the same time there emerged, alongside the existing types, a range of more exotic vessel forms, sometimes elaborately rouletted and/or stamped (Fig. X, nos. 56 and 57, and Plates 30 and 31).

Production of the New Forest colour-coated wares, such as beakers and flagons, also seems to have been established about 260-70, and most of the elaborately painted forms almost certainly belong to before mid IV or a little earlier. Marketing of painted, stamped and incised vessels had probably ceased by *c.* 370 and the industry may well have collapsed by the end of IV.

Crambeck wares, whose manufacture near Malton (North Yorkshire) commenced in the first half of IV, were of comparatively local importance, until the reorganization of supplies after *c.* 367 gave them a large share of the northern military market. Two important products were cooking pots and flanged bowls in a lead-grey burnished fabric (often with an incised internal wavy line) (Fig. XII, nos. 71 and 72), and yellowish-white *parchment ware* bowls (Fig. XII, nos. 73 and 75) with red painted stripes, hooks and scrolls on the flange or interior; the hammer-head and wall-sided mortaria (also sometimes painted) had fine black iron-stone grits (Fig. XII, no. 74).

Argonne ware. A similar but late 'descendant' of samian ware, made in north-east France, reached Britain in very small quantities in IV. The bowls (Fig. XI, no. 70) are distinguished by horizontal bands of impressed patterns (often squares infilled with diagonals), executed with a *roller-stamp,* a roller on which several repeating panels of design had been cut.

Calcite-gritted ware culinary vessels, which had always been quite widespread in the Midlands and north, became particularly popular further south (east of a line from Gloucester to Northamptonshire) in the latter part of IV, and seem to have continued to be made there when production of other wares had ceased in V. Characteristic was a dark 'soapy' fabric, often *rilled* (Fig. V, no. 32), and heavily tempered with particles of shell or natural calcium compounds which sometimes weathered out, leaving a pitted (*vesicular*) effect.

6
Local industries

Some more widely distributed regional types included:

Dales ware. Coarse shell-gritted cooking pots (Fig. XIII, no. 79), from north Lincolnshire or South Yorkshire; late III-IV in the military north, but homeland production begins in the second half of II.

Derbyshire ware. Pimply jars, with a rim-groove to hold a lid in place (*lid-seated*), of mainly IV north of Yorkshire, but II-IV in the homeland, where production probably began in connection with supplies to Little Chester fort (Derby) (Plate 24).

East Midland burnished wares. Grey-brown bowls and jars, with heavy burnishing in bands, from kilns such as Swanpool, Lincoln (IV) (Fig. XIII, nos. 76-78). They formed a major component of the pottery of the north-east Midlands in late III-IV.

Knapton ware. Crude, hand-made cooking-pots, of native origin, heavily tempered with calcite mineral-grits, and with a rectangular outbent rim and a wall slightly concave immediately above a plain flat base. Distribution concentrated mainly in east Yorkshire in III-mid IV. About mid IV or shortly before, there developed from these vessels the well-known *Huntcliffe type cooking pot* (Fig. XIII, no. 80), common on Hadrian's Wall and the Yorkshire coastal signal-stations after *c.* 369; the type probably emanated from a number of centres.

Trent Valley ware. A rough, dark grey, shell-gritted fabric with a rather spongy, bubbly surface, most frequently occurring in tall cooking-pots or jars with corrugated sides and sharply everted rims similar to some Dales ware (see above). Margidunum and Norton Disney (Lincs) are possible production centres.

Parisian stamped wares. (Plate 17). Marketed mainly in Lincolnshire and South Yorkshire (late I to late II).

Savernake ware. Light grey flint-gritted (mid I-II) vessels, mostly jars distributed over north-east and central Wiltshire. Potting probably commenced to supply the army of Mildenhall, Cirencester, and southern Gloucestershire in mid I (Fig. IV, no. 26).

Alice Holt/Farnham grey kitchen wares, sometimes with *combing* or white paint (Plate 25, and Fig. XIV, nos. 82-84), from Hampshire/Surrey and widely distributed over southern England in late III-IV but more locally marketed from late I.

Pevensey ware. A very hard, dark orange-red paste, with an uneven surface, and a deep red-orange colour-coat, occurring in thick late imitation samian forms (Drag. 36, 38, and a bulbous carinated bowl of Oxfordshire type). Decoration mainly comprised white paint, linear rouletting, rosettes, demi-rosettes, or wedge-shape 'herringbone' comb stamps arranged in parallel or diagonally opposed lines. Distribution is limited to the coast of Sussex and east Hampshire, and a floruit of around mid IV is probable.

Many other local varieties of pottery have been recognised including *Congresbury ware* (Avon), *Clapham shelly ware* (Bedfordshire), and *Patch Grove ware* (Kent/Surrey), and regional sources such as Wiggonholt (West Sussex), Highgate Wood (London), the Roxby area (Humberside) and Wappenbury (Warwickshire). Indeed the study of regional and local wares is still in its infancy and offers great potential.

7

The end of the Romano- British pottery industries

Details are obscure, but it seems probable that in the increasingly unsettled conditions of V, when the country split into small self-governing communities, the larger potteries, which were dependent upon a sophisticated monetary system and safe communications to sell their wares, collapsed when such were lacking. Some calcite-gritted wares continued perhaps until *c*. 450. In the eastern half of England hand-made pottery of continental and local origin appears with the Saxon settlers who were arriving in this region from mid IV onwards. In the south and west coarse hand-made vessels often imitating late Roman forms, and made of clay incorporating chopped vegetation (*grass-tempered ware*, Plate 33) appear to have been made from V onwards, but only in small quantities; elsewhere people must have used wood or leather substitutes.

8
Kilns

Much Romano-British pottery was fired in kilns, the best-known exception being black-burnished ware, which was probably baked in surface bonfires or trenches. A typical kiln (Plate 34) consisted of a *stoke-hole* and *flue*, in which the fire was situated, and an adjacent clay-lined *furnace-chamber*, whence the hot air passed upwards through a vented clay floor to an *oven* in which the pots were stacked. The furnace-chamber might contain supports for the *oven-floor* and its load of pots; the whole oven was probably domed or part-covered with clay or turves. T-shaped ovens, of the type normally associated with drying corn in Roman Britain, are now well attested on a number of kiln sites, where they were presumably used for the preliminary drying of pots prior to firing.

More ephemeral types of surface-built kilns — temporary structures with re-usable kiln furniture — have recently been recognised in Essex, the Upper and Lower Nene Valley and elsewhere. They tend to be associated with 'Belgic' style pottery, and often geared to the military markets of mid I.

Further reading

Collingwood, R. G. and Richmond, I., *The Archaeology of Roman Britain*, chaps. xiii and xiv (Methuen, 1969) (very weak on early wares).

Detsicas, A. (ed.), *Current Research in Romano-British Coarse Pottery*, Council for British Archaeology Research Report, no. 10 (CBA, 1973).

Gillam, J. P., *Types of Roman Coarse Pottery Vessels in Northern Britain* (Oriel Press, 3rd edn, 1971). (The author has now modified his views about the dating of pottery of later II and III, and now tends to place material with dates assigned to this period up to 20 years earlier.)

Greene, K. T., *Guide to Pre-Flavian Fine Wares c. AD 40-70* (Cardiff: privately printed, 1971).

Hartley, B. R., *Notes on the Roman Pottery Industry in the Nene Valley*, Peterborough Museum Occasional Paper, no. 2 (reprinted 1972).

Johns, C., *Arretine and Samian Pottery* (British Museum, 1971).

Webster, G. (ed.), *Romano-British Coarse Pottery: A Student's Guide*, Council for British Archaeology Research Report, no. 6 (CBA 2nd edn, 1969) (with extensive references).

Plate 1. Varnished wares (p. 9). *Left:* rusticated cup, ht 4.5 cm. *Right:* cup with applied scales, ht 6 cm (both probably of Lyons origin). *Centre:* cup with applied barbotine, probably of Spanish origin, ht 7 cm (Copyright: British Museum).

Plate 2 (below left). Buff mica-dusted jar with pressed-out 'bosses', a form typical of mid I, ht 14.7 cm (p. 9) (Copyright: British Museum).

Plate 3 (below right). Lead-glazed flagon with relief-moulded decoration, probably of Allier origin (p. 9), ht 14 cm (Copyright: British Museum).

Plate 4. Bowl imitating samian form Drag. 37, with greenish lead-glaze over white-painted decoration, probably a Holt (Clwyd) product (p. 9), ht 16.5 cm (Copyright: British Museum).

Plate 5. Gallo-Belgic wares (p. 10). *Top left:* pedestal cup, ht 11.5 cm. *Top centre:* butt-beaker, ht 18.5 cm. *Top right:* Terra Nigra cup, diam. 13.5 cm. *Bottom left:* Terra Rubra platter with potter's stamp, diam. 17.7 cm. *Bottom right:* stamped Terra Nigra platter, diam. 19.2 cm (all mid I) (Copyright: British Museum).

Plate 6. Poppy-head beaker or jar with panels of barbotine dots, late I to early II, ht 17.7 cm (p. 12) (Copyright: British Museum).

Plate 7. Samian bowl with relief-moulded decoration incorporating the stamp (retrograde) of the important manufacturer CINNAMVS of Lezoux, c. AD 140-75, diam. 25.8 cm (p. 10) (Copyright: British Museum).

Plate 8 (top). Fragment of a mould for the manufacture of a Drag. 37 samian bowl, made by Lezoux potter DRUSUS I (X-3), *c*. 90-110, diam. 21.5 cm (p. 10). (RCHM [Eng] : Crown Copyright).

Plate 9 (above). Samian ware (p. 10) *Left:* Drag. 36 bowl with barbotine decoration, diam. 13.2 cm. *Right:* Drag. 33 cup, diam. 10.1 cm, both Central Gaulish, second-century (Copyright: British Museum).

Plate 10. London ware bowl (p. 11) imitating samian form Drag. 30 with incised lines and compass-scribed semicircles, ht 12·7 cm (Copyright: British Museum).

Plate 11. Black-burnished ware (p. 13). *Top:* cooking-pots with obtuse-angled lattice, ht (left to right) 18 cm, 22 cm, and 28 cm. *Bottom left and right:* flanged bowls, diam. 18 and 15 cm. *Bottom centre:* dog dish, diam. 20 cm. (Current Archaeology).

Plate 12. Mortarium with incomplete retrograde stamps CANDIDVS and FECIT impressed on either side of the elaborate protruding spout; the potter CANDIDVS almost certainly worked at Brockley Hill (Greater London) *c.* AD 95-135; ht 7.7 cm (p. 14). (Copyright: British Museum).

Plate 13. Cast of scene from the Igel Monument (Germany) depicting a basement kitchen; in the centre a servant pounds food in a *mortarium* (with spout to his right) set in a special frame; to the left, vessels are being washed in a trough and metal platters are stacked on edge; on the right servants are cooking food over a stove (mid III) (Rheinisches Landesmuseum, Trier).

Plate 14. Rusticated ware cooking-pot, ht 13·5 cm (p. 12) (Copyright: British Museum).

Plate 15 (above left). Face-pot with red painted stripes on the body; the female mask would have been made in a mould, probably a fourth-century Crambeck product, ht 25.5 cm (RCHM[Eng.] : Crown Copyright).

Plate 16 (above right). Amphora (p. 10) with stamp on rim, first century, ht 113.5 cm. (Copyright: British Museum).

Plate 17. Parisian ware stamped jar, ht 18.5 cm (p. 21) (RCHM [Eng.]: Crown Copyright).

Plate 18 (below left). Nene Valley colour-coated 'hunt cup' with relief of a dog chasing a hare applied *en barbotine*, ht 10.7 cm (p. 16) (Copyright: British Museum).

Plate 19 (below right). Colour-coated beaker (lower part restored) of Colchester manufacture with the lively scene of a four-horse chariot race depicted *en barbotine;* the potter may well have never seen such a spectacle since he has depicted the charioteer clad in gladiatorial armour, ht 14.7 cm (p. 17) (Copyright: British Museum).

Plate 20. Nene Valley colour-coated wares (p. 16). *Left:* globular jar with white-painted foliage, ht 12·3 cm. *Centre:* indented beaker with applied scales, ht 15·3 cm. *Right:* bag-shaped beaker with *barbotine* foliage, ht 11·5 cm (Copyright: British Museum).

Plate 21. Nene Valley mortarium with reeded flange and typical black iron-stone trituration grits, III-IV from kiln site at Stibbington (Cambridgeshire), diam. 27 cm (p. 16). (Copyright: British Museum).

Plate 22. Colchester products (p. 17). *Top left and centre:* rough-cast beakers, ht 11.8 and 12 cm. *Top right:* rouletted beaker, ht 12.3 cm. *Bottom left:* jug with white-painted decoration, ht 23.7 cm (all colour-coated). *Bottom right:* flagon with pinched pouring lip, ht 20.5cm. (Copyright: British Museum).

Plate 23. Rhenish ware motto beaker with VIVATIS ([Long] life!) applied in white paint over the colour-coat, ht 11.5 cm (p. 17) (RCHM [Eng] : Crown Copyright).

Plate 24. Derbyshire ware cooking-pot (p. 21). Note the 'pimply' fabric-texture especially on the 'dished' interior of the rim, ht 20.5 cm (Derby Museum).

Plate 25. Alice Holt/Farnham wares (p. 22). *Left:* cooking-pot with white slip and 'combed' exterior surface, late IV, ht 18.4 cm. *Right:* bead-rimmed storage jar, a type with origins in the local pre-Roman Iron Age, ht *c.* 30 cm (Guildford Museum).

Plate 26. Oxford 'parchment ware' bowls with painted decoration (p. 18). *Left and right:* diams. 25.5 cm. *Centre:* diam. 8.5 cm, all from the kiln site at Churchill Hospital, Headington (David Carpenter: Oxford Archaeological Excavation Committee).

Plate 27. New Forest 'parchment ware' bowl with painted decoration (p. 19), diam. 26 cm (K. Grinstead).

Plate 28. Oxford red colour-coated wall-sided mortarium (reconstructed) with 'bat's head' spout, imitating samian form Drag. 45, diam. 16·7 cm (p. 18) (K. Grinstead).

Plate 29. Oxford 'parchment ware' mortaria, late III to early IV, all *c*. 23 cm diam., from Headington kiln site (p. 18) (David Carpenter: Oxford Archaeological Excavation Committee).

Plate 30. New Forest forms (p. 19). *Léft:* 'parchment ware' jar, ht 8 cm. *Centre:* coarse ware flagon, ht 19·5 cm. *Right:* ovolo-stamped late imitation samian bowl, diam. *c.* 14 cm. (K. Grinstead).

Plate 31. Late imitation samian bowl-fragments showing method of impressing rosettes and demi-rosettes directly on to the vessel. *Left:* New Forest ware, rosette diam. 1·4 cm. *Right:* Oxford ware, demi-rosette, diam. 1.5 cm (K. Grinstead).

Plate 32. New Forest fine colour-coated wares (p. 19). *Left to right:* jug with finger-depressed spout, late IV, ht 14.7 cm; globular beaker with incised decoration, ht 14.4 cm; flanged-neck flagon with white-painted panels, ht 19 cm; beaker with 'stabbed' decoration, ht 8.7 cm (all late III-IV); indented beaker with white-painted fronds, ht 15.5 cm (K. Grinstead).

Plate 33. Fragment of grass-tempered ware (p. 23) showing typical surface concavities where vegetation and seeds incorporated in the fabric, have burnt out during firing. *c.* 3 cm across (K. Grinstead).

Plate 34. Reconstruction of a kiln partially loaded for firing, with part of the dome and clay vent-holed oven floor cut away to show 'pilaster' floor-supports projecting from clay furnace-chamber wall; the stoke-hole and stone-reinforced flue lie to the left—a kiln type common in the New Forest (Drawn by N. Griffiths).

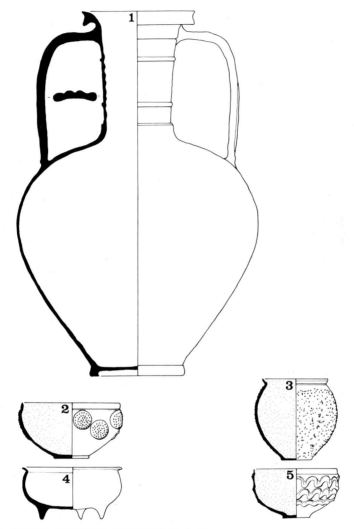

Fig. 1. EARLY IMPORTED POTTERY. Scale ¼.

1. Hofheim flagon (p. 11). Note the pronounced foot-ring and squarish-angled handles (after Anthony).

2-5. *Varnished ware* (p. 9).

2. Lyons cup with applied 'raspberry roundels'.

3. Lyons rough-cast beaker.

4. Tripod bowl (after Cunliffe): Lyons ware.

5. Lyons cup with barbotine 'meanders' (after Atkinson).

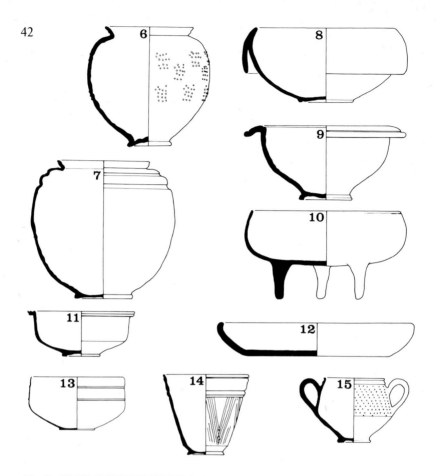

Fig. II. FIRST-CENTURY VESSELS. Scale ¼.

6-11. *Mica-dusted wares* (p. 9). *c.* 43-75; many of these forms occur in other fabrics.

6. Jar with barbotine dots (after Frere/Wilson).

7. Cordoned jar. Note the typically early almost upright everted rim (after Frere/Wilson).

8. Flanged bowl.

9. Bowl with reeded rim (after Frere/Wilson).

10. Tripod bowl (after Frere/Wilson).

11. Carinated bowl (p. 12) with reeded rim (after Hawkes and Hull).

12. 'Imitation *Pompeian red ware*' dish with red slip on interior (*c.* 43-75); the form occurs in other fabrics.

13. Bowl in *egg-shell ware* — such exceptionally thin-walled grey vessels were imported in mid I from Italy and later imitated (after Hawkes and Hull).

14. Incised brown lead-glazed cup (p. 9) imitating samian form; late I; probably a Chichester product (after Down and Rule).

15. Greenish lead-glazed Allier cup (p. 9) with barbotine dots (*c.* 43-70) (after Bushe-Fox).

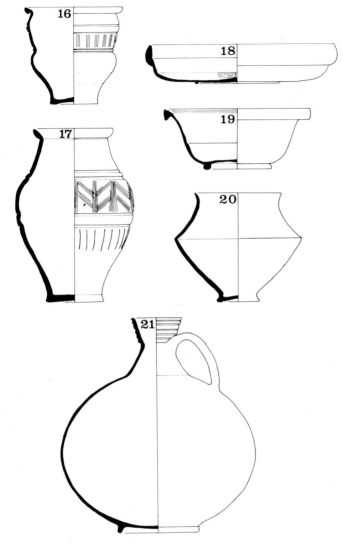

Fig. III. FIRST-CENTURY POTTERY. Scale ¼.

16-20. *Gallo-Belgic wares* (p. 10).

16. Girth-beaker with incised decoration *c.* 43-60 (after Hawkes and Hull).

17. Butt-beaker in typical pale fabric with lightly incised decoration; mid first century.

18. Terra Nigra platter with foot-ring and internal illiterate potter's stamp.

19. Terra Nigra cup (after Hawkes and Hull).

20. Gallo-Belgic derived *biconical* beaker.

21. Ring-neck flagon (p. 11), mid first century form. Note the even, almost vertical rings (after Farrar).

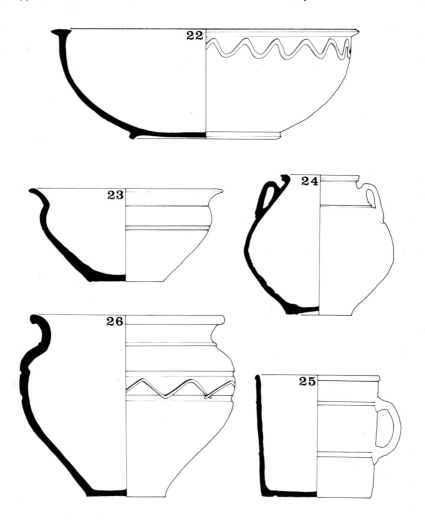

Fig. IV. Scale ¼.

22-25. *Severn Valley wares* (p. 12).

22. Glevum ware bowl. Note the characteristic inward-projecting rim, late I (after Green).

23. Bowl, second half of II (after Webster).

24. Glevum ware 'honey jar', first century (after Green).

25. Glevum ware tankard. Note the basal groove—a feature common to many tankards (after Green).

26. *Savernake ware*, jar (p. 21)—a late I-II vessel form with its neck and body cordons (after Annable).

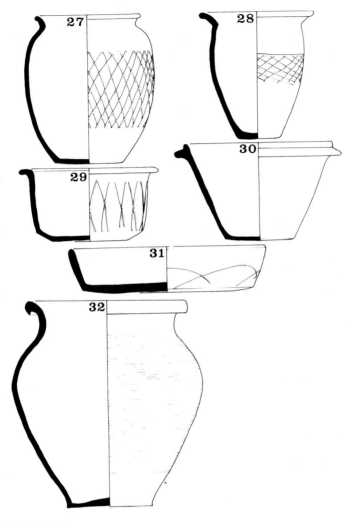

Fig. V. Scale ¼.

27-31. *Black-burnished ware* (p. 13).

27. Second-century cooking-pot (after Farrar).

28. Cooking-pot typical of late III-IV (after Farrar).

29. Second-century bowl (after Farrar).

30. Bowl typical of late III-IV (after Farrar).

31. 'Dog-dish' (after Farrar).

32. Rilled *calcite-gritted* cooking-pot (p. 20) with triangular undercut rim—(typical of IV and early V), a predominantly southern form (after Brodribb, Hands, and Walker).

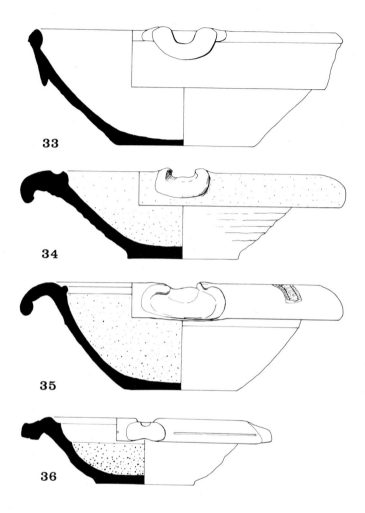

Fig.. VI. FIRST AND SECOND-CENTURY MORTARIA. Scale ¼.

33. Imported mid I form characterized by a *wall-side,* a thick moulded lip, a narrow spout, and a lack of grits (after Hawkes and Hull).

34. Early south-eastern mortarium (p. 14) probably from Kent with level bead-rim and drooping flange typical of *c.* 55-75 (after Cunliffe).

35. Mortarium from Verulamium kilns (p. 14) with retrograde stamp of the potter LALLANS; the rather hooked flange and internal bead are typical of *c.* AD 90-130 (after Woods/Turland).

36. 'Raetian' mortarium (p. 15), (a Wilderspool product) with lug handles, red-brown slip and brown grit, *c.* 160-200 (after Gillam).

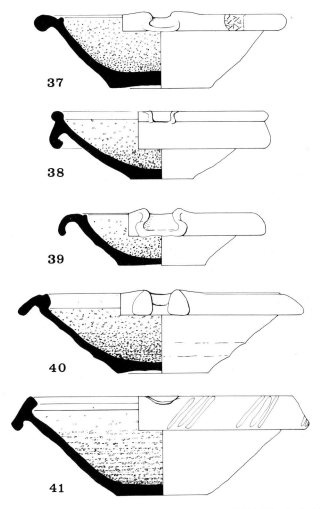

Fig. VII. OXFORD AND HARTSHILL/MANCETTER MORTARIA. Scale ¼.

37. Oxford mortarium (p. 15) from Cowley with illegible potter's stamp on rim *c.* 120-60 (after Atkinson).

38. Oxford mortarium of late II to early III. Note the more prominent bead rim, almost vertical flange, and simpler spout (after Woods/Turland).

39. Hartshill/Mancetter mortarium (p. 14) with small bead rim and hooked flange typical of mid II (after Steer).

40. Hartshill/Mancetter mortarium with more swollen bead rim and splayed flange typical of late II (after Birley).

41. Hartshill/Mancetter mortarium with *hammer-head* rim (p. 15) decorated with red-brown paint, late III-IV.

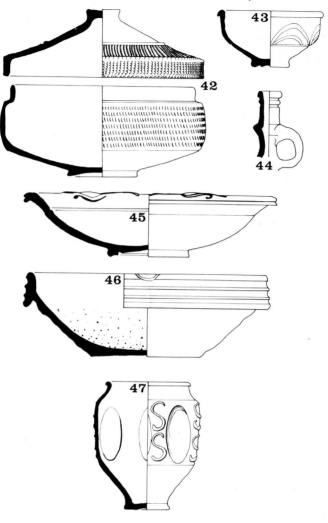

Fig. VIII. NENE VALLEY PRODUCTS (p. 16). Scale ¼.

42. Colour-coated castor box and lid, late II-IV; these tend to be larger than their Colchester equivalents (Fig. IX, no. 48) (after Hartley).

43. Colour-coated bowl with cream painted arches (after Hartley).

44. Flanged-neck of colour-coated flagon; late III to early IV (after Hartley).

45. Colour-coated dish imitating samian form Drag. 36, with barbotine leaves, third century (after Hartley).

46. Mortarium with reeded rim, late III-IV (after Hartley).

47. Colour-coated indented beaker with barbotine scrolls, late II to early III (after Woods/Turland).

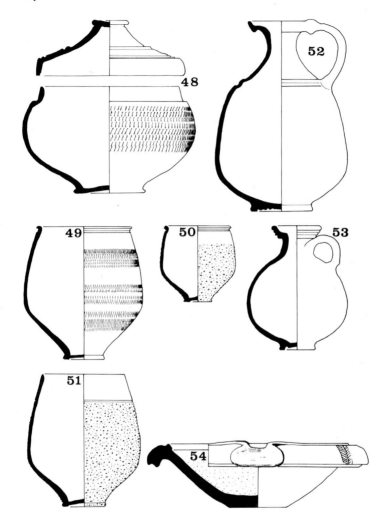

Fig. IX. COLCHESTER PRODUCTS (p. 17). Scale ¼.

48. Colour-coated rouletted bowl with matching lid, second century (after Hull).

49. Colour-coated bag-shaped beaker with cornice rim; the zones of rouletting are typical of mid II (after Hull).

50. Rough-cast colour-coated beaker with cornice rim, mid II (after Hull).

51. Rough-cast colour-coated beaker with simple rim, mid II (after Hull).

52. Flagon imitating metal prototype, late II (after Hull).

53. Ring-neck flagon with cup-shaped mouth typical of II (after Hull).

54. Mortarium with herring-bone trademark stamp, mid II (after Hull).

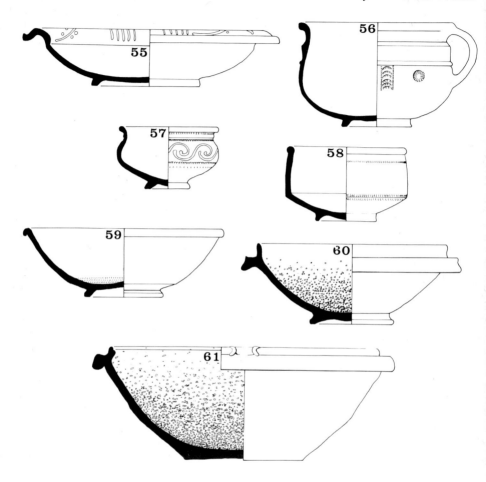

Fig. X. OXFORDSHIRE PRODUCTS (p. 18). Scale ¼.

55. Late imitation samian dish (Drag. 36 variant) with white paint on rim (after Bushe-Fox).

56. Late imitation samian bowl with impressed rosettes, demi-rosettes and comb-stamping (after Bushe-Fox); second half of IV+.

57. Late imitation samian bowl with rouletting and white painted decoration; the neck-cordon is typical of many Oxford vessels: c. 330+.

58. Late imitation samian rouletted carinated bowl; mid IV+.

59. Late imitation samian rouletted bowl (Drag. 18/31R) (after Wheeler).

60. Red colour-coated mortarium with prominent bead-rim and angular flange typical of IV.

61. Cream mortarium with prominent bead-rim and 'rolled over' flange typical of late III-IV.

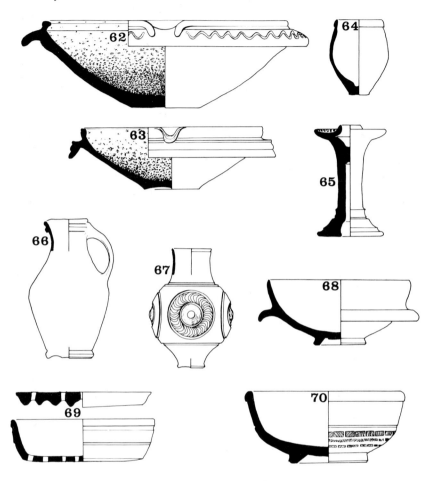

Fig. XI. Scale ¼.

62-69. *New Forest Wares* (p. 19).

62. 'Parchment ware' mortarium with incised decoration, late III to mid IV.

63. Mortarium with reddish colour-coat and typical fourth-century bead-rim and reeded flange.

64. 'Parchment ware' jar, fourth century.

65. 'Parchment ware' candlestick with red painted decoration, late III-IV.

66. Colour-coated jug with depressed lip, late IV.

67. Colour-coated globular beaker with incised and painted medallions; late III to early IV.

68. Late imitation samian flanged bowl, form Drag. 38: fourth century.

69. Coarse ware cheese press and matching lid.

70. *Argonne ware* bowl (p. 20) with roller-stamped geometric decoration.

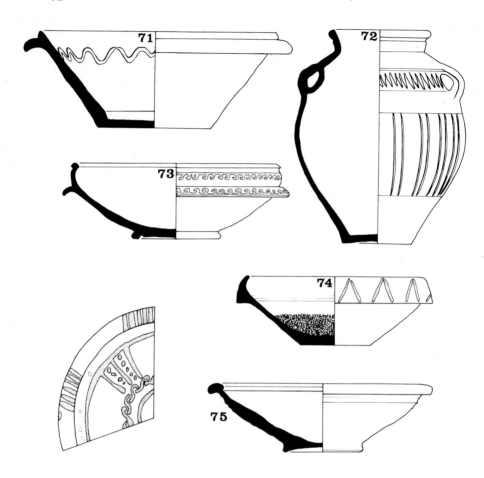

Fig. XII. CRAMBECK PRODUCTS (p. 20). Scale ¼.

71. Grey ware flanged bowl (after Corder).

72. Grey ware cooking-pot; the form was probably manufactured at other northern centres (after Corder).

73. 'Parchment ware' bowl with red-painted 'hooks' (after Gillam).

74. Yellowish-white mortarium with red-painted decoration; this simple wall-sided form of late IV developed from the Crambeck hammer-headed form of mid IV (after Mitchelson).

75. Bowl in 'parchment ware' tradition with elaborately painted internal decoration (left) (after Wacher).

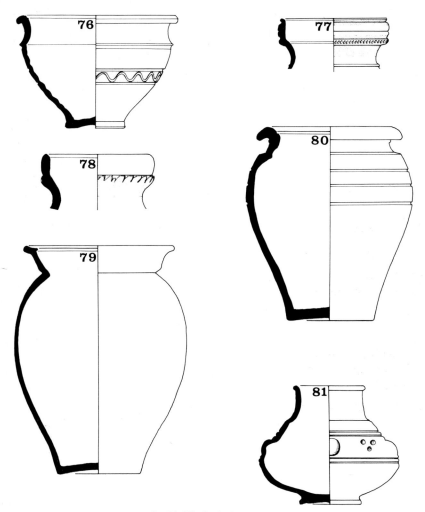

Fig. XIII. LOCAL WARES (p. 21-22). Scale ¼.

76-78. *East Midland burnished wares* (p. 21).

76. Bowl with burnished line (after Todd).

77. Narrow-mouthed jar with notched collared rim (after Todd).

78. Narrow-mouthed jar with 'frilled ' collared rim (after Todd).

79. *Dales ware* cooking-pot (after Gillam).

80. *Huntcliff-type cooking-pot:* a calcite-gritted vessel common in the north.

81. *Romano-Saxon ware:* a regional native style of pottery employing 'bosses' and 'dimples' and largely confined to eastern England where it occurs in a number of fabrics in late III-IV (after Myres).

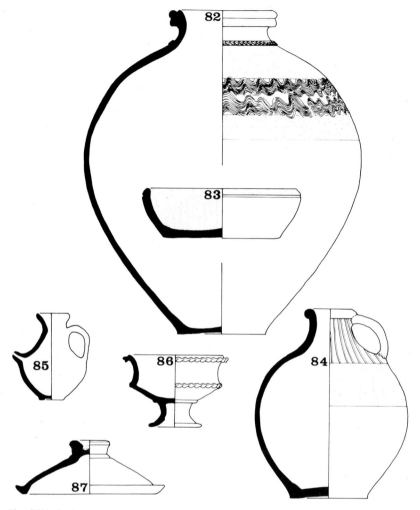

Fig. XIV. Scale ¼.

82-84. *Alice Holt/Farnham wares* (p. 22).

82. Storage jar with areas of white paint (stippled) and combed decoration; fourth century (after Clark).

83. Dog dish with white-painted area—a popular form; fourth century (after Clark).

84. Flagon with burnished decoration—a common southern form; late III-IV.

85-87. *Types of vessels.*

85. *Lamp-filler,* often called a 'tettina.'

86. *Tazza* or incense cup in pale fabric with pedestal and frilled bands.

87. Lid for cooking-pot or jar.

Museums

Those listed have extensive Roman pottery collections, but are only a *regional* selection; in addition many local museums both in towns and on actual Roman sites contain relevant displays. *Perhaps the best way to learn and handle pottery is to volunteer to wash and mark it for an excavation or museum,* since the difference in appearance between surface finds of weathered sherds and freshly excavated unabraded pottery can be quite remarkable.

Cambridge. University Museum of Archaeology and Ethnology, Downing Street.

Canterbury. Canterbury Royal Museum, High Street.

Cardiff. The National Museum of Wales, Cathays Park.

Carlisle. Tullie House Museum and Art Gallery, Castle Street.

Chester. The Grosvenor Museum, Grosvenor Street.

Cirencester. The Corinium Museum, Park Street.

Colchester. Colchester and Essex Museum, The Castle.

Dorchester. Dorset County Museum, High Street West.

Edinburgh. The National Museum of Antiquities of Scotland, Queen Street.

Gloucester. Gloucester City Museum and Art Gallery, Brunswick Road.

Leicester. The Jewry Wall Museum, St Nicholas Street.

Lincoln. Lincoln City and County Museum, Broadgate.

London. The Museum of London, London Wall, EC2.

Newcastle upon Tyne. The University Museum of Antiquities, The Quadrangle.

Oxford. The Ashmolean Museum of Art and Archaeology, Beaumont Street.

Peterborough. The Peterborough Museum and Art Gallery, Priestgate.

Reading. The Reading Museum and Art Gallery, Blagrave Street.

St Albans. The Verulamium Museum, St Michael's.

Salisbury. Salisbury and South Wiltshire Museum, St Ann Street.

Shrewsbury. Rowley's House Museum, Baker Street.

Winchester. Winchester City Museum, The Square.

York. The Yorkshire Museum, Museum Street.

Index